Jack Up!

A farce
Ian Hornby

New Theatre Publications - London
www.plays4theatre.com

The edition published in 2013

New Theatre Publications

2 Hereford Close | Warrington | Cheshire | WA1 4HR | 01925 485605

www.plays4theatre.com   email: info@plays4theatre.com

New Theatre Publications is the trading name of the publishing house that is owned by members of the Playwrights' Co-operative. This innovative project was launched on the 1st October 1997 by writers Paul Beard and Ian Hornby with the aim of encouraging the writing and promotion of the very best in New Theatre by Professional and Amateur writers for the Professional and Amateur Theatre at home and abroad.

ISBN 9 781 840 94905 6

Cast *(see note below)*

Alex - *Abbeywood supporter*
Bobby - *Abbeywood supporter*
Chris - *West Worth supporter*
Joe - *West Worth supporter*
Sam - *Abbeywood captain*
Nick - *Abbeywood player*
Nat - *West Worth player*
Les - *West Worth captain*
Pat - *policeman/woman*

Important Notes
Every character in this play can be cast as a man or a woman (in any mix), and they can be of any age. The names, as far as possible, are gender-free, but may be changed as wished (for example Joe might become Jo if played by a woman.

Place names may be changed to local place names if wished.

Synopsis of Scenes

ACT I Scene 1 - *Saturday afternoon, 5pm*
ACT I Scene 2 - *the following Thursday, late evening*
ACT II Scene 1 - *one hour later*
ACT II Scene 2 - *the following Saturday afternoon, 4pm*
Epilogue - *half an hour later (very short scene)*

Copyright Information

Video-Recording of Amateur Productions

Performing Licence Applications

A performing licence for these plays will be issued by "New Theatre Publications" subject to the following conditions.

Conditions

1. That the performance fee is paid in full on the date of application for a licence.
2. That the name of the author(s) is/are clearly shown in any programme or publicity material.
3. That the author(s) is/are entitled to receive two complimentary tickets to see his/her/their work in performance if they so wish.
4. That a copy of the play is purchased from New Theatre Publications for each named speaking part and a minimum of three copies purchased for backstage use.
5. That a copy of any review be forwarded to New Theatre Publications.
6. That the New Theatre Publications logo is clearly shown on any publicity material. This is available on our website.

Fees

Details of script prices and fees payable for each performance or public reading can be obtained by telephone to (+44) 01925 485605 or to the address below.

Alternatively, latest prices can be obtained from our website www.plays4theatre.com where credit/debit cards can be used for payment.

To apply for a performing licence for any play please write to New Theatre Publications 2 Hereford Close, Warrington, Cheshire WA1 4HR or email info@plays4theatre.com with the following details:-

1. Name and address of theatre company.
2. Details of venue including seating capacity.
3. Dates of proposed performance or public reading.
4. Contact telephone number for Author's complimentary tickets.

Or apply directly via our website at www.plays4theatre.com

Jack Up!
A comedy by Ian Hornby

Suggested set (minimum)

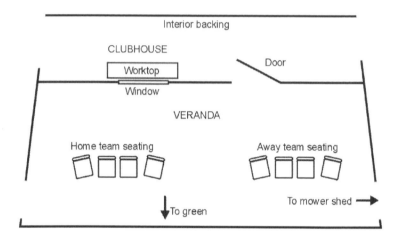

The play is set on the verandah of a green bowling club pavilion. At the rear of the stage is the clubhouse itself, and the dividing wall should have one door and one or more windows looking directly out over the green. Downstage is the verandah itself, which will, at various times, house chairs, tables, scoring tables and so on as needed. An artist's impression of a simple set is on the previous page, though we want the window to be see-through rather than reflect the green so that the goings-on inside the clubhouse can be seen. Both door and windows should be functional. It is possible to enter and exit L and R in front of the line of the clubhouse.

The edge of the auditorium is the edge of the green itself. Ambitious theatres may wish to add green carpet or false grass down the centre aisle and actually bowl for real.

The play is deliberately flexible in terms of gender and age, such that most characters can be played by men or women, as desired, and age is largely unimportant.

ACT I Scene 1

It is midway through a bowling match between the home club, Abbeywood Bowling Club, and their rivals, West Worth Bowling Club.

There are lines of chairs on the verandah, facing the audience, at which sit Alex and Bobby, the Abbeywood supporters, stage R, and CHRIS and DANNY, West Worth supporters, stage L, all holding scorecards and pens, with small wooden boards to support the scorecards and a bulldog clip to keep each in place. A table stands near the clubhouse door US. There is a money box or collection box on the floor L. Bowls and bags are on the floor around them. The door and windows to the clubhouse are open, as befits the summer's day. Sam enters from the clubhouse. From the rear of the hall, FRANCIS (Abbeywood) and Nat (West Worth) enter.

Nat	*(calls to Joe)* How much am I short?
Joe	You ought to know, you're closer to it than the jack is. Bowl up, for God's sake!
Nat	Not helpful, Joe; we're all trying.
Sam	How's he doing?
Alex	Last end, either way.
	(Nick holds up one finger on each hand.)
Sam	Looks good.
Alex	*(looking towards Nick)* Two? That's game! *(Marks card and detaches it from the board.)*
	(All clap as Nick and Nat walk to the stage carrying their bowls, a jack and a mat. They shake hands as they get close.)
Nick	Well played. I thought I had you there.
Nat	Same here. You were unlucky. Shame it couldn't have been a draw, eh? Well played anyway.
	(Both mount the stage to congratulations from their own supporters. They turn L and R towards their own supporters. The next few lines sotto voce.)
Bobby	Well played, Nick.
Chris	*(who is rather deaf)* What? Speak up.
Bobby	*(louder)* I said well played, Nick.
Chris	Yes. Well played Nick.
Joe	Well played, Nat.

Alex/Chris	*(together)* Good game?
Nick	No, he a cheat. Glad I won.
Nat	No. He cheated. Otherwise I'd have won.
Bobby/Joe	*(together)* It's playing that counts.
Nick/Nat	*(together)* No, it's winning that counts.
Sam	*(to the Abbeywood crowd)* Amen to that. Still, I suppose I'd better do the sporting diplomacy thing. *(Walks across to Nat and offers hand.)* Hard luck old man. I thought you'd got that one. Just as well for us. That puts us one ahead.
Nat	*(shakes hand)* Still, it's the playing that counts.
Sam	Yes, that's the spirit.
	(Both gravitate back to their supporters.)
Sam/Nat	*(together, sotto voce)* Bastard!
Chris	*(holds out a charity collection box)* Come on then, Nat. 20p.
Nat	Not sure I have any cash.
Chris	You know the rules - you lose a game and 20p goes towards the West Worth development fund.
Nat	*(manages to find change in pocket, puts it in box.)* There we are. Though we're not going to get much development done at 20p a game.
Joe	It all helps.
Nat	*(pointedly)* Perhaps our *(sarcastic)* friends at Abbeywood would like to add a little to our collection.
	(The Abbeywood team turn away and pretend the haven't heard.)
Nat	Didn't think so. Mean buggers.
Alex	Better get the opposition a cuppa, Sam.
Sam	Acid, more like.
Alex	You are the captain. Last think you need is them to report you to the Association.
Sam	I suppose. *(Walks back towards Nat.)* Fancy a cuppa, old man?
Nat	*(a tiny but suspicious)* Er... Yes, don't mind if I do. In here? *(Indicating clubhouse door.)*
Sam	Don't worry. Sit and watch our win. Enjoy the sunshine. I'll

	get it. Milk and sugar?
Nat	Please.

(Sam goes towards the clubhouse while Nat sits with his team mates, who are watching an imagined game on the green. Sam watches from the doorway. As they watch they concentrate, all three leaning to stage L as if trying to influence the wood in. Meanwhile the Abbeywood supporters are leaning the other way, trying to steer it out. Eventually - milk the tension here, cast - it is success for West Worth, to the "yes, yes" delight of their own supporters and the groaning disapproval of the Abbeywood contingent. This timing should be well rehearsed to achieve maximum impact. West Worth supporters clap enthusiastically, Abbeywood reluctantly - and slowly - applaud because they think they should. The contrast between the two sets of applause and expressions can be used to good effect.)

Chris	*(calling)* Great wood, Ken. One more and it's game.
Nat	*(feeling better)* Any time with the tea, Sam. *(False smile.)*
Sam	*(with bad grace)* Coming right up. *(False smile. As he moves towards the clubhouse door)* And I hope it chokes you.
Nat	*(sotto voce)* And I hope it scalds you.

(Sam goes in the clubhouse, appearing in front of the window, with an implication the work top with the tea on is directly in front of the window, so we can see him working.)

Nat	*(sits with his own team and looks at the score sheets)* How're we doing?
Chris	Couldn't be closer. Neck and neck.
Sam	*(calling though the window)* Did you say sugar, Nat?
Nat	*(focussed on score sheets)* Please. Two.
Sam	*(evilly)* Right. *(Rubs his hands together and we see him add a large number of sugars to the tea, eventually emptying the entire container in.)* Coming up!

(Sam enters through clubhouse door carrying a tray with the cup and saucer with teaspoon and a plate of biscuits/cakes. He moves to Nat and hands over the tea, then moves towards his own team, very obviously keen to

watch how Nat reacts to the tea. Nat tastes it and immediately works out what Sam has done, but refuses to give him the satisfaction of seeing any reaction.)

Nat   Very nice, thanks. Did you put sugar in?

Sam   *(disappointed his joke hasn't worked)* Probably needs stirring.

Nat   Good point.

(Nat picks up his spoon and stirs the tea. Sam, disappointed, stops watching and goes to his team. It is obviously some effort for Nat to stir all that sugar, and in the end his gives up, the spoon standing vertically in the cup - this could be achieved by jamming a piece of polystyrene in the cup beforehand, or maybe rice in the bottom of the cup.)

Sam   Well?

Nat   Good point. *(Tries it.)* Perfect.

(Sam, annoyed, turns away. Nat pours the tea in Chris's bowls bag, which has been preciously modified with a suitable container inside.)

Alex   *(looking out)* Oh no. He can't...?

Bobby   *(looking out)* What?

Alex   Les... He's going to strike.

Sam   What!? Take cover everyone.

Nat   What's the problem?

Sam   Er... Nothing. Nothing. *(Disappears inside clubhouse.)*

Alex   Les... Don't do it!

Bobby   *(cringing)* Too late. Look out!

(The Abbeywood team shield their faces as the West Worth team looks out and sees what's about to happen. All look on agog. Sam is looking out gingerly from the clubhouse window.)

• Sfx - clatter as the bowl strikes something.

(All the spectators look on as something sails up in the air in front of them. There is the crash of broken glass backstage and Sam disappears below the window.)

Nat   *(sneers to green)* Missed!

(Sam, looking dazed, enters from the clubhouse, his head

	and shoulders covered in debris and holding the offending bowl.)
Alex	I wish he wouldn't do that. He never hits anything.
Bobby	Apart from that bump in the green, you mean? He gets that every time.
Alex	That must be the fourth skylight we've lost this season.
Sam	Fifth.
Nat	*(to the Abbeywood team)* You should issue a health and safety warning.
Joe	Shhh! Last end. Whoever gets this, wins.
Chris	Is it that close?
Joe	Closer. *(Shouts)* Come on Ken! *(Starts to clap and chant)* Ken…! Ken…! Ken…!
	(Chris and Nat join in.)
Chris/Nat	*(clapping and chanting)* Ken…! Ken…! Ken…!
Sam	*(outraged)* Do you mind!? This is a crown green bowling club, not a… a… Hooligans' club!
Chris	*(aside)* Oh, I don't know.
	(They carry on chanting.)
Alex	Disgraceful behaviour!
	(They chant louder. The Abbeywood team stare in silent disbelief.)
Sam	*(eventually; calls)* Les…!
	(All stare in disbelief. The West Worth team start their chant again.)
Chris/Joe/Nat	Ken…! Ken…! etc.
Sam	*(louder; calls)* Les…! Les…! Les…! *(Rallies the others.)* Les…! Les…! Les…!
Alex/Bobby	*(joining in with Sam and clapping)* Les…! Les…! Les…!
	(It becomes a contest. It falls silent as the player bowls. Repeat of the leaning business above, except this time they lean the other way. Finally, cheers from West Worth and more groans from Abbeywood. They all look at the score sheets.)
Sam/Nat	*(together)* I don't believe it. A tie.
Alex	What? On points scored?

Chris	Yes. The points scored are exactly the same. 5 games each (not that that matters in this league) and equal on points.
Joe	So who wins the league?
Nat	Neither of us. We have to play the match again.
	(All are aghast. Groans all round.)
Sam	Again? Oh God!
Alex	Then all this stress has been for nothing?
Bobby	Looks like it.
Nat	*(rises and goes to Sam.)* Well, old man, I wish I could say well played.
Sam	*I* don't. Your lot cheated.
Nat	*Ours* did? Your lot did, you mean!
Sam	I don't want to discuss it.
Nat	Typical. *(Returns to seat, picks up a cake from the tea things and throws it at Sam.)*
	(The teams retaliate until it becomes a bunfight. Eventually Nat and Sam emerge and approach each other downstage while the rest are still fighting.)
Sam	A week's time, then…?
Nat	A whole week. *(With total lack of sincerity)* I can't wait.
	(Lights fade as the mayhem continues in the darkness and then fades also.)

ACT I Scene 2

Scene	the same, two days before the rematch, late evening. The general lighting is now dark (and grows darker over the course of the scene). Alex and Bobby are sitting on their seats, this time with blankets on their laps to counter the evening chill.

● SFX - *A portable radio plays some night music softly.*

Alex	Turn that row off, Bobby.
Bobby	It keeps me calm.
Alex	It has the exact opposite effect on me. And we'll have the neighbours complaining.

Bobby	*(rises and turns off the radio.)* OK, OK... I get the message!

● SFX - *radio off*

Alex	Did you bring your torch?
Bobby	*(removes tiny torch from pocket and shows it.)* I got some spare batteries too. *(Flicks it on and shines into the auditorium.)*
Alex	Call that a torch? What are we going to see with that?
Bobby	You've got a better one, I suppose?
Alex	I have. *(Goes in clubhouse and returns with a huge torch.)* Now this is a torch. 3.5 million candlepower.
Bobby	No idea what mine is.
Alex	One, I'd say. Then again a candle would probably be brighter. *(Clicks the switch on the big torch. Nothing happens.)*
Bobby	I think I'll stick with mine.
Alex	Just needs charging, that's all.
	(Sam enters carrying three mugs of coffee, which he hands out. He has a camera round his neck.)
Bobby	Not *more* coffee?
Sam	Helps keep us awake.
Bobby	This must be the tenth tonight.
Sam	Leave it then! Bloody ungrateful.
Bobby	I was only saying... *(This is a habitual saying of Bobby's when stressed. Puts coffee down.)* What exactly are we looking for?
Sam	Anyone strange wondering about. Up to no good.
Bobby	By *anyone* you mean West Worth players?
Sam	I mean anyone. They may be conniving buggers but they're not stupid. They'll probably get someone else to do their dirty work so they're not recognised on our video surveillance cameras.
Alex	We don't have any video surveillance cameras.
Sam	You know that... I know that... But they don't.
Alex	So what...?
Sam	I may have let it slip just as they were leaving after the

	match the other day.
Alex	And you're hoping they believe you?
Sam	Why not? Anyway, just keep your eyes open.
	(They peer out at the "green" and all is silent for a few minutes, during which they sip their coffee.)
Sam	Going to be a cold one, I think. Fancy something to warm it up?
Alex	Such as?
Sam	*(reaches in pocket and brings out a bottle or flask of vodka.)* Russia's finest. Bobby?
Bobby	Not for me, thanks. Need to keep a clear head.
Sam	Alex?
Alex	If it's good enough for the Kremlin… *(Looks at bottle, which has no label and looks dubious.)* You sure this is Russian?
Sam	Well, no… And it's more gin than vodka… Well spotted, actually. *NickFrancsizek* would give you a better description.
	*(Note "**Francsizek**" is a Polish name, pronounced "**<u>Fran cee shek</u>**", though a clumsy English version could be used if the characters wish.)*
Alex	Not heard of that brand at all. Polish, isn't it? Same name as our greensman as a matter of fact.
Sam	Yes. He runs a nice sideline from the mower shed.
Alex	*Our* mower shed!?
Sam	Shhh. Keep your voice down. Very few people know, you know.
Alex	That's because it's totally illegal.
Sam	Only if someone finds out. I grabbed a bottle from the shed earlier.
Alex	You sure it's safe?
Sam	'course it is. Same as any other booze… Except this is made from grass cuttings.
Alex	What!?
Sam	*Francsizek* reckons it's a shame to waste them. An old polish recipe, he says. Try it. It's not bad if you hold your

breath.

Alex   Just a small nip then.

(Alex shakes head and holds out mug. Sam gives them both a good dash, leaving Bobby's coffee as it is.)

Sam   That'll take the edge off.

Alex   *(takes a sip and reacts)* Phew! That's powerful stuff. How many proof is it?

Sam   Ah, now I know a bit about alcohol proof. You take the ABV - that's alcohol by volume, multiply by 7 and divide by four. That gives you the percentage proof.

Alex   How come you know that?

Sam   Scottish parents with a keen interest in distilleries. *(Uses calculator on mobile phone.)* So if you took 50% ABV that works out at 87.5% proof.

Alex   And what d'you reckon *Francsizek's* is?

Sam   *(sips and considers)* About 200.

Alex   Lend me your phone. *(Takes phone; presses buttons.)* Hang on a sec. If 50% ABV is 87.5% proof, that means 100% ABV is 170% proof.

Sam   Yep.

Alex   So *Francsizek's Special Brew* is more than 100% alcohol? That's impossible.

Sam   Taste it again before you say that.

Alex   *(sips again; hoarse)* Yes, OK, I take your point. Just as well we've got the coffee to dilute it.

Sam   I wouldn't risk it otherwise. Cheers!

(They sip the coffee and look out.)

Alex   D'you think this is all this really necessary?

Sam   The vigil? Yes, it is. I don't trust that lot.

Alex   But we've been doing this all week. And there's not been a sign of a West Worth invasion.

Sam   Only a couple of days to go then. They're probably out there *(peers out across the "green")*, just waiting for us to slip up, to take our eye off the bowl…

Bobby   I think you're just a worrier. They're rational people, just like us. What d'you expect them to do?

Sam   Look, you've been a member here as long as I have.

Bobby   So?

Sam   In all those years, how many times have you seen a molehill?

Bobby   Never have, as far as I can remember.

Alex   Nor me.

Sam   Don't you think it's strange, then, that since the tied match we've had three?

Bobby   I was only saying…

Alex   What are you suggesting?

Sam   That those buggers from West Worth have set moles free on our green, deliberately.

Bobby   Can you do that?

Sam   They could.

Alex   But why would they? They have to play on the green too, remember.

Sam   Rule 9a - if the home green is unfit to play, the away green is used.

Alex   I don't remember that rule. And I was secretary at my old club.

Sam   You wouldn't where you come from - it's a local amendment.

Bobby   *(hopefully)* Maybe West Worthless won't know about it either. *(Rises.)* Scuse me, need the loo. All that coffee isn't good for me. *(Exits into clubhouse.)*

Sam   I bet they do. Otherwise why would they be sabotaging our green?

Alex   We've no proof they are, yet.

Sam   Yet. But we will. Hence this vigil. We spot one of them doing anything, take a photo and bingo - they forfeit the match. Probably get drummer out of the league, too.

Alex   You dislike them that much?

Sam   More.

Alex   Why?

Sam   I used to be married, you know. Until my wife saw their bloody chairman in his posh uniform. That was it; she was

	smitten. Bastards.
Alex	Your wife went off with the West Worth chairman?
Sam	No need to go on about it.
Alex	Did she bowl?
Sam	For the County. To be honest, that's what I'm most annoyed about. We'd have won the league if she'd been playing. As a wife, she wasn't that good... but as a bowler... wow!
Alex	I wonder what's keeping Bobby?
Sam	Probably fallen asleep. Miserable bugger.
Alex	Maybe you should liven his coffee up too.
Sam	What?
Alex	*Francsizek's Revenge*?
Sam	Good idea. *(Puts a very large dash of vodka in Bobby's mug.)*
	(Pat, in police uniform, appears through the auditorium, shining a torch towards the stage.)
Pat	Hello? Somebody there?
Sam	*(squinting against the light)* Who's that?
Pat	What's going on here, then?
Alex	It's the Police!
Sam	It's Pat. Local bobby. Always snooping round. *(Calls)* Here, Pat... you're wondering all over the green in your great big boots.
Pat	Never mind all that. What're you lot doing?
Sam	Keeping watch on the green... In case of sab... *(thinks better of the word "sabotage)* ...vandals.
Pat	That's *our* job Sir. Why don't you get off home to bed?
Sam	Can't take the chance. We've got a needle match coming up.
Pat	And that means you're expecting vandals?
Sam	Yes.
Pat	*(suspicious)* I see. Well, I can do without all this. I'm off on my holidays in the morning.
Alex	Oh, yes? Anywhere nice?

Pat	A cruise. The Caribbean… Sun and sea for two whole weeks. Anyway, about these vandals…
Alex	*(quickly)* We've had a spate of damage to the green surface, you see, officer?
Pat	Which you reported to the Police, of course?
Alex	Ah, no…
Pat	*(matter-of-fact; more a statement than a question)* No.
Alex	There didn't seem much point, really. I mean you've got more important things to do.
Sam	*(sotto voce)* Like hounding speeding motorists and so on.
Pat	I heard that sir.
Sam	Well, shouldn't you spend more of your time catching killers?
Pat	It so happens, sir, that motorists kill far more people than *killer* do.
Sam	That may be so, but…
Pat	Which means you are far more likely to be sent bowling in the next world by a drunk driver than a serial killer.
Sam	Er, yes. *(Has a wicked idea.)* Can we offer you a mug of coffee, officer? *(Picks up Bobby's mug and holds it out.)*
Pat	Expecting someone else, are we?
Alex	*(quickly)* No. Sam poured too many. And it *is* a cold night after all.
Sam	Or aren't you allowed to drink on duty?
Pat	That only applies to alcohol, sir. Don't mind if I do. *(Accepts the coffee and starts to drink.)* So have you seen any sign of your vandals?
Alex	Not so far.
Pat	Probably just youngsters, you know. A few beers inside them and they go a bit wild.
Alex	Yes, probably.
Pat	I see some things on my rounds, I can tell you. Most of it to do with booze or drugs. Never touch the stuff myself.
Alex	Very wise.
Pat	Never have, never will.
Sam	Drugs, you mean?

Pat	Never would try drugs, that's for sure.
Sam	But alcohol in moderation…?
Pat	*(dubious)* Well… Alcohol in moderation…
Alex	A sensible amount…
Pat	Reluctantly, I suppose. But in my case I have an allergy to it.
	(Sam and Alex exchange glances.)
Sam	An… allergy?
Pat	They're not sure whether it's an allergy or just intolerance. So I never touch the stuff. Never.
Alex	Good idea.
Pat	I suppose I've become intolerant in a couple of ways. I don't really approve of booze at all, if I'm honest.
Sam	Er… How does it affect you? When you've tried it I mean?
Pat	I get very warm, then come out in a rash and eventually pass out, usually.
Alex	*(gulps)* Pass out?
Pat	Well, when I say "usually", the last time I had any I did.
Alex	You want a fresh cup of coffee? That must be cold by now.
Pat	No, it's fine. No worries. *(Drains mug.)* Warmed me up a treat, that has. *(Starts to itch.)* Anyway, about your vandals.
Alex	You're right. We should probably go home and leave it to you.
Sam	Nonsense, I want to catch them at it.
Alex	*(a hiss)* Sam…!
Pat	And what will you do when you find these *vandals*?
Sam	Take their photos and send them to the League. *(Proudly shows his camera.)*
Pat	The *League*? You mean us…? The *Police*?
Sam	Did I say "league"? Yes, I meant "Police", of course.
Pat	Meanwhile I think I'll take a look around, just in case. Phew, that really has warmed me up. *(Continues to scratch.)* Can I use your loo before I go?

Alex	Sure… Help yourself.
	(Sam and Alex look uneasily at each other as Pat exits to the clubhouse.)
Sam	What are we going to do?
Alex	Not much we can do, is there?
Sam	We just have to hope he gets fed up and goes off to pass out somewhere else.
Alex	I can't believe we gave a vodka laced mug of coffee to an alcohol-intolerant copper!
Sam	Well, we can't undo what's done.
	(There is a crash from inside the clubhouse. Both turn to face it as Bobby rushes out, pointing inside and unable to find his voice. He carries a bowling wood.)
Alex	Oh God.
	(Bobby is still waving his arms, wildly pointing to the clubhouse.)
Sam	Yes, we know. A policeman has passed out in the toilet.
Bobby	*(shakes head, then looks at them mystified. Eventually finds his voice)* A policeman!? Oh God.
Alex	He passed out from alcohol intolerance.
Bobby	No… he passed out from a wood on the head.
Alex	What?
Bobby	*(to Alex; holds up the wood)* Your wood, in fact. It was handy.
	(Alex and Sam rush inside, coming out moments later with stunned faces. Bobby puts the wood down on a table.)
Bobby	I thought it was an intruder coming to get me. It was self-defence, honestly.
Sam	I'll look forward to the judge's face when you explain that in court.
Alex	Didn't you notice the uniform?
Bobby	No, it's very dark in there and I left my torch out here.
Sam	We'll be done for assaulting a police officer.
Alex	We? Don't rope me in on this. It was Bobby who dealt the fatal blow.
Bobby	*(in panic)* Fatal? Is he dead?

Alex	Figure of speech.
Sam	We're all in it. I brought the vodka, but just went along with it.
Alex	Oh, thanks.
Bobby	Of course it's always possible he's not a policeman at all.
Alex	What!? You *are* joking?
Bobby	Could be someone *pretending* to be the Police.
Alex	You're delusional.
Bobby	I was only saying… It's possible.
Alex	Don't you start.
Bobby	I was only saying it's possible.
Sam	Well, it isn't. I recognise him.
Alex	You really think West Worth would go to the trouble of hiring an actor and a police uniform just to sabotage Abbeywood?
Sam	*(emphatically)* I would if the situation was reversed.
Alex	You're seriously sad.
Sam	*(squaring up)* Says who?
Alex	*(up for the challenge)* Says me!
Bobby	*(intervening)* Please…! Please…! We can't afford to be arguing while we've got an unconscious policeman in the clubhouse.
Alex	If you hadn't been such an idiot we wouldn't *have* an unconscious policeman in the clubhouse!
Bobby	It's not my fault!
Sam	Well it's not mine.
Alex	I hope you're not suggesting it's mine!?
Sam	It's more yours than mine!
Bobby	I hit him accidentally. What you did was deliberate!
Alex	OK, enough, enough. It's none or our faults and it's all our faults. Whatever. It doesn't change what's happened.
Bobby	I was only saying… *(Pause.)* So what are we going to do? What if someone comes?
Sam	*(a sneer)* Like who?
Alex	*(thinking)* Like a member of the West Worth club? Like

	you were suspecting?
Sam	If they come and try to sabotage our green they'll get the same treatment as PC Plod in there!
Alex	They wouldn't need to sabotage our green any more. One look at what we've done and they'll be on to the papers before you can call *Pat Up*! Once the League finds out, it's all over.
Bobby	God, yes!
Alex	We have to stop them finding out.
Sam	How?
Alex	We have to hide him.
Bobby	Hide him!? Where?
Sam	We could use the back room... where we keep the equipment... Or the shed...
Alex	And what do we do with the mowers?
Sam	Good point.
Alex	It's obvious!
Sam	It is?
Alex	Of course. We don't hide him at all... We sit him out here, with us. That way we can keep an eye on him and we appear to have extra troops if West Worth launch an offensive.
Sam	*(unsure)* It could work...
Alex	(warming to the idea) Of course it could. It will mean we have to hide him during the day, but we can take the mowers out during the day like we always do.
Bobby	What if he wakes up?
Alex	Ah, yes, didn't think of that... How much vodka have you got left?
Sam	Plenty. Why, you need a refill...? *(Realises Alex's intentions.)* No, we can't. We just can't!
Alex	It's either that or another bang on the head with your best wood.
Sam	Couldn't we use a jack?
Alex	Got any better ideas?
Sam	(shakes head) No.

Alex	*(to Bobby)* You?
Sam	No, I suppose not.
Alex	Right! Let's get him out here. I've got a blanket in my car; we can use that to cover him up.
Sam	It's look like he's dead!
Alex	I don't mean completely covered, just across his lap. Keeping out the cold, you know. I'll go and get it. You go and bring out your dead.
Bobby	I wish you wouldn't keep saying things like that.
	(Sam exits through the clubhouse door, followed by Alex and Bobby, who return a few moments later helping the semi-conscious Pat to a chair.)
Pat	*(slurred)* What's going on? What happened?
Sam	Don't you worry about that
Pat	Where am I?
Sam	Er… You're on a cruise ship in the Caribbean.
Pat	Lovely. *(Pause.)* Why is it so dark then?
Sam	Er… because the sun's so bright.
Pat	Sun… right. Can't see the sun. *(Tries to stand but is very unsteady, going from side to side.)*
Sam	Just relax. Listen to the sea. *(Indicates for Bobby to help.)*
	(Bobby makes sea noises and imitates gulls.)
Sam	And the fish calling.
Bobby	*(sotto voce)* They're seagulls!
Sam	And the seagulls.
Bobby	*(impersonates a waving palm tree.)* Look, the palm trees are waving in the warm breeze. *(Makes swishing noises.)*
Pat	*(swaying and staggering)* Sea's a bit choppy today.
	(Sam picks up Pat's sway and goes along with it, urging Alex and Bobby to do the same, which they do, as if in rough seas.)
Sam	Yes, choppy. Up and down… up and down…
Pat	*(suddenly feels unwell)* I think I'm going to be sick.
Alex	You come and sit down on this… deck chair. You'll be fine.

Bobby	Deck chair?
Pat	Deck chair... Yes.
	(They help Pat to a chair.)
Alex	Better now?
Pat	Much, thanks. Ah, this is the life! *(Settles back, then notices the uniform and looks puzzled.)* Why am I dressed in police uniform?
Sam	Er... The fancy dress party! In the main ballroom! You remember!
Pat	Ah, yes, fancy dress party. I remember. *(Pause.)* No, I don't remember. I don't remember anything. All I remember is...
Sam	Yes?
Bobby	Oh, heck.
Pat	I musht've been sitting under a palm tree when we went ashore. I remember a great big coconut falling on my head.
Bobby	*(picks up wood, holding it just above Pat's head.)* Like this one?
	(Alex enters, carrying a blanket.)
Pat	Yesh. Jush like that. *(Comes to a little more, but still slurring)* Hang on a minute! Bowling club... Vandals...
	(Bobby bops him on the head with the wood - this could be feigned or a padded police cap could be worn. Pat is knocked out again.)
Alex	What did you do that for?
Bobby	He started to remember. I panicked.
Alex	Well *don't* panic!
Sam	Is he still breathing?
Bobby	Of course... I hope.
Alex	Put that wood down before you really kill someone!
Bobby	It's supposed to be a coconut.
Sam	Well put it down! Now!
	(Bobby puts the wood back on the table as Alex checks Pat is still alive.)
Sam	What about a police car?

Bobby	What about one?
Sam	He may have left one parked outside.
Alex	It'll be a good deterrent from West Worth's answer to the SAS then.
Sam	And also a very good pointer to anyone who's looking for a missing copper.
Alex	Good point. Bobby, go and see. If there's one there, move it.
Bobby	Me!?
Sam/Alex	*(together)* You!
Bobby	But I've been drinking.
Sam	No you haven't. He had yours. That's another reason all this is your fault. If you didn't have a weak bladder *you'd* have drunk the vodka and not the law. No go and move the car.
Bobby	I was only saying… *(reluctantly)* I suppose I… *(Exits.)*
Alex	Help me get him up straight.
	(They start to arrange Pat in the chair, wrapped in a blanket and looking asleep, having to have several attempts because each time they think they've done he topples over, mumbling about coconuts.)
Bobby	*(returns)* Keys! I need the keys!
	(They all fumble in Pat's pockets until they find the keys. This means they have to go through the rearranging business afresh.)
Sam	Phew! *(Sits down.)*
Alex	Yes, phew! *(Sits.)*
Sam	Top up? *(Pulls out flask/bottle.)*
Alex	May as well.
Sam	*(tops up their mugs.)* Cheers.
Alex	I can't believe we're doing this. We've kidnapped a copper.
Sam	We had no choice, right?
Alex	Someone's bound to start searching.
Sam	It's only a couple of days.
Alex	Is that supposed to help?

Sam	A couple of days and we'll put him in the car and drive it somewhere. We'll leave the bottle in the car and it's look like he was boozing and had a reaction.
Alex	We can't do that!
Sam	Why not? From the way he was behaving before, he can't remember a thing.
Alex	So we ruin an innocent copper's career by planting a bottle of booze?
Sam	Desperate time, old man. Cheers!
Alex	*(glum)* Yes... Cheers!
	(Both drink. Bobby returns, looking dazed.)
Sam	Moved it?
Bobby	Er... Sort of.
Sam	Sort of? Well did you or didn't you?
Bobby	I moved it, yes...
Alex	But...?
Bobby	I didn't move it far.
Sam	Why not?
Bobby	I misjudged it. It was dark, you see, and I thought switching the lights on might wake the neighbours.
Alex	And...?
Bobby	And I drove into a ditch.
Sam	I don't believe it! You prat.
Bobby	It wasn't my fault. I'm only qualified to drive automatics.
Sam	God, help us.
Alex	You should have said!
Bobby	I didn't like to. I'd have been breaking the law and you...
Alex	has it occurred to you that knocking out and kidnapping a copper is a bit more serious than driving a manual car?
Bobby	I bet I'm not insured, either. Unless police cars are insured for anyone to drive. That would make sense, wouldn't it? It would mean that if someone found a police car they could return it without breaking the law and...
Sam	Shut up, Bobby!
Bobby	I was only saying that...

Alex	Shut up, Bobby!
Bobby	You're blaming it all on me again, aren't you…?
Alex/Sam	*(louder)* Shut up, Bobby!
Bobby	I could do with a drink.
Sam	We can't spare it. We'll need it if Plod wakes up. It's a bit more subtle than two and a half pounds of Lignum vitae!
Bobby	What?
Alex	It's the wood they make bowling woods from. Though a lot of them are composite these days.
Sam	We don't need a lesson in how to make bowls!
Bobby	Alex was only saying…
Sam	I don't suppose it matters what they're made of in terms of their ability to induce concussion!
Alex	What are we going to do about the Panda car?
Bobby	We could phone the AA.
Sam	The motoring organisation or Alcoholics Anonymous?
Bobby	Or the RAC. I wonder if the Police are members.
Sam	Were you born stupid, or did you just develop badly?
Bobby	I was only saying…

● Sfx - car horn off

(All start.)

Alex	*(nervous)* Who the hell's that?
Sam	*(nervous)* I hope it's not the police.
Bobby	*(casual)* No… Probably the pizza man.
Alex	The… pizza… man…?
Bobby	I ordered a Hawaiian.
Alex	You did what?
Bobby	Sorry. Did you want one?
Sam	*(in disbelief)* You… ordered a pizza? At this hour?
Bobby	I was hungry. It's OK, I don't mind sharing. It's a supersize. No anchovies, though. I hate anchovies.
Alex	Do they *have* anchovies on Hawaiians?
Sam	Where did you find a pizza place open at this time of night?

Bobby	That Greek one behind the petrol station.
Alex	Not sure I'd want to eat anything from there.
Bobby	Because it's Greek?
Alex	No, because it's filthy. Anyway, that bloke's no more Greek than I am.
Bobby	Gregor?
Alex	Gregor? I bet his name's Bert or Fred.
Sam	*(losing patience)* Does it matter? Does it *really* matter? Haven't we got more important things to worry about?
Alex	*(after a pause, a shake of head and a sigh)* Go and see if it's your pizza, then.
Sam	And *don't* invite the guy in!
	(Bobby exits.)
Sam	I often wonder whether Bobby exists in a different universe.
Alex	Come to think of it, though, pizza sounds very good at the moment. Didn't realise how hungry I was till Bobby mentioned pizza.
Sam	I don't feel like I've eaten for a week. Or slept, come to that.
Alex	Tell me something… Is winning the league that important?
Sam	Definitely. Especially against West Worth.
Alex	Like I said, I'm new here. Why the rivalry?
Sam	*(starts to answer, then stops, thoughtful)* D'you know, I can't remember?
Bobby	*(returning)* Anyone got change for a twenty?
Sam	I haven't even got a twenty.
Alex	I think I may have. *(Fishes in pocket and takes out notes. Holds out two five pound and one ten pound notes.)* These do?
Bobby	*(looks askance)* I mean twenty pee.
Sam	You want change of 20p? Why?
Bobby	It's exactly ten pounds. I always give the guy a tip. But 10p is quite enough.
Sam	*(tosses Bobby two 10p pieces from his pocket.)* Last of the big tippers, eh?

Bobby	*(genuinely)* They deserve it; coming out at this time of night. Thanks. *(Exits.)*
Sam	Now *that* is mean.
Alex	Anyway, you were saying…
Sam	Was I?
Alex	About the old rivalry?
Sam	Been going on as long as I remember. I wonder if anyone actually know why? On either side?
Bobby	*(returns, carrying a pizza box)* I do.
Sam	Enthral us.
Bobby	Well… *(Opens box.)* Hell… anchovies. I hate anchovies. They taste like salted fish.
Sam	That's because they *are* salted fish.
Bobby	*(picking out anchovies)* Are they…? That explains it then.
Pat	*(snores and wakes - kind of)* Where am I? I can smell fish.
Sam	Saint Lucia.
Pat	Is it time for a swim?
Sam	No, time for sleep.
	(Sam sings a lullaby; encourages the other two to join in. Pat eventually goes back to sleep.)
Alex	We really should move him. If you're right and one of the West Worth lot do come round, the last thing we need them to see is a sleeping policeman. *(Don't substitute "policewoman" here - it won't work.)*
Bobby	It would slow them down a bit.
Sam	Excuse me?
Bobby	A sleeping policeman… One of those bumps in the road that slows you down.
Alex	This is no time to be making jokes, Bobby.
Sam	And that was no joke.
Alex	Where can we hide him?
Bobby	I know! The mower shed! Behind the cricket pitch. Nobody ever goes in there.
Alex	*(awkward glance at Sam)* No! We can't put him in there.
Bobby	Why not? Francsizek's got the week off, so it's ideal.

Alex	But the...
Sam	*(interrupting quickly)* ...the mower's in there. There's no room. We'll put him in the toilet.
Alex	That could be inconvenient.
Sam	Don't *you* start making jokes!
Alex	I wasn't. I meant it. If anyone *does* come to call... and they happen to need the loo... the game would be up.
Sam	Good point.
Bobby	So it has to be the mower shed. Come on... I'll give you a hand.
Sam	*(rather too quickly)* No...! Alex and I will do it. You go and see if you can move the police car.
Bobby	I told you... it's got two wheels in the ditch.
Sam	*(snaps)* Well try! Get some planks and put them under the wheels!
Bobby	Planks? Where am I going to find pl... I know... the mower shed! *(Starts towards the exit.)*
Alex	*(quickly stops Bobby moving; calmly)* Bobby... You go out and assess the damage and we'll bring you some planks out when we're finished with our stowaway. There's some wood in the store room.
Bobby	But...
Sam	Now, Bobby!
Bobby	OK, OK. I'm going!

(Sam and Alex watch Bobby exit through the clubhouse door.)

Alex	What was all that about?
Sam	We can't have Bobby seeing Francsizek's still. The fewer people that know about that, the better, especially Bobby. He never could keep a secret. Come on, give me a hand.

(Sam and Alex lift Pat under the arms and drag him off L. Pat sings "A Life on the Ocean Wave" as they go. When then have gone, Les - the West Worth captain - appears through the auditorium and walks to the stage shining a torch.)

Les	*(looking round)* Hello? Anyone here? (Continues looking round the area, ending up stage R, facing away from the

	Clubhouse door. Sam returns through the clubhouse door, followed closely by Alex, carrying a couple of lengths of wood, stopping dead when they see someone there.)
Sam	*(sotto voce)* Wait! Get back… *(Holds Alex back.)* I knew it!
Alex	What?
Sam	We have a visitor. Hell, it's Les.
Alex	Who?
Sam	The West Worth captain. I bloody knew they'd try something.
Alex	What're we going to do?
Sam	Leave this to me! *(Steps bravely out from the door and grabs Les's shoulder.)* Gotcha!
Les	*(turns, matter-of-fact)* Oh, hello, Sam.
Sam	Don't you *hello, Sam* me. You've been caught red-handed.
Les	I have?
Sam	What were you planning? Weedkiller on the green? Moles? Dandelions?
Les	What *are* you talking about?
Sam	Thought you could win the League by sabotage, did you? We'll, we've got your number, Les. And don't try anything. I've got backup *and* witnesses.
Les	To what…? Sam, what are you talking about?
Sam	*(starting to be dubious)* What exactly are you doing here?
Les	We had a report of an abandoned police car outside.
Sam	*(gulps)* We…? Abandoned… police… car…?
Les	Yes. About an hour ago.
Sam	What's that got to do with you?
Les	Everything. Didn't you know? I'm the Assistant Chief Constable for the area.
Sam	You are? Oh sh… *(quickly corrects)* should have remembered that.
Les	I happened to be on my way home when a report of the car came through, so I said I'd drop in and take a look.
Sam	Very… community-minded of you.

Les	I came in across the cricket field - nothing there. Better check the road, I suppose.
Sam	*(quickly)* There's no police car out there. We'd have noticed. *(Quickly indicates to Alex to go out.)* Nor any missing police officers.
	(Alex takes the planks and exits.)
Les	Missing police officers? Who said anything about missing police officers?
Sam	Ah... Well, stands to reason, doesn't it? Abandoned police car? Someone must have driven it here... I mean to wherever it was abandoned. So chances are that police officer hasn't checked in.
Les	Good point. But they never said anything about a missing officer.
Sam	It's the only explanation.
Les	Don't you believe it. I wouldn't put it past the local criminals to nick a car from the station and go for a joy ride.
Sam	Yes... Never thought of that.
Les	But they're bound to leave prints. We'll get them.
Sam	But, on the other hand, it could be one of your lot.
Les	West Worth?
Sam	No, not local criminals... the police.
Les	If one of them's sloped off to the pub and is lying up drunk somewhere...
Sam	*(gulp)* Drunk?
Les	I'll have his guts for garters.
Sam	Or hers.
Les	Yes. Or hers. The only one I can think of would be Pat. You know Pat?
Sam	Yes. Our local bobby.
Les	But he's on holiday. I think. Tenerife.
Sam	*(before thinking)* Caribbean cruise. Or maybe Peterborough
Les	Really?
Sam	But not till the morning.

Les	Oh yes? How did you know that…?
Sam	I er… I think it may have come up in conversation.
Les	Tonight? You've seen…?
Sam	No… Days ago. Weeks maybe.
Les	Hmm… *(Pause.)* So you've not seen anything?
Sam	Not us. And we're been here all night.
Les	Why, as a matter of interest?
Sam	Keeping watch on the green… In case of… vandals.
	(Pat, staggering, appears in the doorway. Sam distracts Les so he doesn't see Pat.)
Les	You should have called us.
Sam	No, you have enough to do. We can keep watch.
	(Alex and Bobby appear in the doorway, dragging Pat back out again. Bobby puts hand across Pat's mouth, resulting in a muffled moan. They drag Pat off.)
Les	*(turns, but too late)* What was that?
Sam	What was what?
Les	I thought I heard someone. *(Moves towards clubhouse door.)*
Sam	A fox, probably. We get them lots round here. Anyway, you were saying… *(Easing Les back down centre.)*
Les	Just make sure you aren't taking the law into your own hands.
Alex	Message received and understood. Roger wilco and all that.
Les	So, have you seen any vandals?
Sam	Only you.
Les	Excuse me?
Sam	I mean, you're the only person we've seen.
	(Alex reappears.)
Sam	Isn't that true, Alex?
Alex	What is?
Sam	We've not seen anyone. Everything's quiet out there, isn't it? No abandoned police cars or anything?
Alex	All cleared up.

Bobby	*(enters)* I dumped it down the road. *(Stops dead on seeing Les.)*
Alex	*(quickly)* The dregs from the coffee pot. It clogs our drains...
Sam	So we pour it down the grid...
Alex	Down the road.
Les	You've got coffee?
Alex	Er, yes... Want one?
Les	Wouldn't say no. A bit chilly tonight.
Alex	In the clubhouse. Follow me.

(They all troop into the clubhouse and we see them cross the window to stage R. Moments later Pat appears, swaying and carrying two bottles of booze.)

Pat *(slurs)* You'll never guess what they gave me at the bar... Free booze! Yippee! Oh, nobody on deck!

(Pat moves downstage and trips, ending up propped against the back of one of the chairs.)

Pat *(as in "Titanic", giggling)* I'm flyingggg"! *(Unsteadily makes the chair. Slides into the chair, trying to stay upright. Drunkenly)* Captain... we're sinking...! Abandon ship! Abandon ship! *(Giggles, then slowly passes out as the lights fade.)*

End of ACT I

Interval

ACT II Scene 1

Scene - the same - one hour later.

Les, Bobby and Alex are sitting on the seats chatting. Sam appears from the clubhouse carrying a tray and four mugs. There is a bowls jack and a mat on the chair DL - the one Pat will end up sitting on. Pat's mobile phone is out of sight under the chairs.

Sam Right! Coffee! You said no sugar, right, Les?

Les Yes. I've got some sweeteners somewhere. *(Checks pocket.)*

Sam	Watching the weight, eh? *(Sits.)*
Les	*(depending on actor/actress size)* Hardly. *(or)* Always.
Bobby	All we seem to have done all night is drink coffee. It's given me a headache, to be honest. And I never get headaches with coffee.
Alex	Unfamiliar brand, I expect. *(To Sam)* Sam, are these...? *(Meaning "laced with booze".)*
Sam	Pure as the driven snow, mate. *(Shakes head and points, unseen, to Les's and Bobby's coffees.)*
Les	You've still not told me why you're here in the middle of the night.
Sam	Yes we did. Vandals.
Les	Ah yes. Vandals. A bit vague, though, isn't it?
Alex	How d'you mean?
Les	Well, have you had anything vandalised so far?
Alex	Well, no, but...
Les	So what makes you think you will now? Or do you spend every night of the year here.
Sam	*(together)* Yes. *(Beat.)* No!
Alex	*(together)* No. *(Beat.)* Yes.
Sam	Drink your coffee, Les. It'll help you sleep.
Les	I don't want to sleep. If you feel the need to keep watch then I'll help.
Sam	Help...? Us...?
	(Les's mobile phone rings. He answers it.)
Les	Excuse me... Hello...? *(Pause.)* Yes..., Terry...? Where...? So it was dumped near here... He's what...? *(Meaning Pat.)* Tried his mobile...? Right, I'll keep my eyes open. Keep me informed.
Alex	Problems?
Les	They found the police car. Crashed into a lamp-post. Just in the next street, actually.
	(Alex and Sam glare at Bobby.)
Bobby	It was an accident, OK?
Les	How do *you* know?
Bobby	Er... How do I know...? Well...

Sam	Must have been. Otherwise we'd have heard the ambulance.
Les	Ambulances go to accidents.
Alex	Yes, but if it had been serious they'd have had sirens on.
Sam	Yes.
Bobby	Yes.
Les	Probably not at this time of night... Anyway, it was empty.
Bobby	Good.
Les	Good?
Bobby	Nobody was hurt then?
Les	No, it was being driven by Pat - you know him?
Sam	*(together; quickly)* Yes. *(Beat.)* No!
Alex	*(together; quickly)* No. *(Beat.)* Yes.
Bobby	*(after a delay)* No.
Sam	Local community officer, yes?
Les	That's the one.
Alex	Yes... That's the one. OK, is he?
Les	No idea. He's gone missing.
Sam	See? I mentioned missing police officers before, didn't I?
Les	*(suspicious)* Yes... You did. D'you know anything about this?
Sam	Of course not, do we?
Alex/Bobby	No.
Sam	Just good deductive reasoning. I always wanted to be in the Police. I'd have made a good detective.
Les	I'm just worried that with the car being found near here...
Bobby	*(dramatically)* Maybe he's been abducted by aliens.
Alex/Sam	Shut up, Bobby!
Bobby	*(sulky)* I was only saying...
Sam	Well don't just say!
Bobby	*(takes over, imagination running riot.)* He could have seen the vandals and gone chasing after them, then, swerving round a corner on two wheels, tyres screeching as they fought to grip, he lost control at the last seconds and...

Sam	Yes, thank you, Bobby.
Bobby	*(in full flow)* …and crashed into the lamp post, leaping out of the car in case it was electrified and continuing the chase on foot. The gang realised they outnumbered him and turned, and now they're holding him for ransom in an abandoned dockside warehouse with a timer ticking away on a home-made dynamite bomb. There'll be a ransom note in the morning, you mark my words.
Sam	Have you finished?
Bobby	Yes… I think so. I was only saying…
Alex	I think you watch too much television.
Bobby	It could have happened like that…
Sam	But we know… *you* know… it wasn't like that at all, was it?
Bobby	It wasn't?
Sam	In all probability the police officer went for a walk to check a shop, or a factory…
Alex	*(dry)* or a bowling club…
Sam	…and while away, some idiot tried to move the police car. Some complete, incompetent, stupid idiot.
Les	I told the station to keep trying the mobile. He's not answering it for some reason.
	(At that moment Pat's mobile phone rings. All look at each other. It is a very common, ordinary ring.)
Sam	*(quickly)* Ah… That's my phone. I'd recognise that ring tone anywhere. Now where did I put it?
Alex	Sounds like it's coming from over there. Help me find it, quickly.
	(All stand and move over to where the phone is hidden.)
Sam	*(to Les, turning him back)* No, not you. You just sit and relax… You're a guest.
Les	I don't mind helping.
Sam	Please, I insist. We insist… We don't want your coffee going cold, do we?
	(As Sam occupies Les, he passes a flask of the moonshine gin to Alex, who, unseen by Les, pours a generous measure into Les's coffee.)
Les	Very well… If you insist.

Sam	Oh, we do… Don't we?
	(Nods from the others.)
Alex	*(finds the phone and hands it to Sam.)* Here! *Yours* I believe.
Sam	Thanks. *(Clicks a button so the ringing stops.)* Hello…? Yes… darling… *(awkward glance and a smile to Les)* No, darling…, *(a general statement.)* Yes, darling…? *(A question.)* No, darling…! *(Shock.)* Yes, darling… *(calm agreement.)* Yes… Bye, darling. *(Hangs up.)*
Alex	Who was it?
Sam	Wrong number.
Les	What?
Sam	Just a joke. My daughter. Wants to know if I want a meal when I get in.
	(The phone rings again.)
Les	Persistent, isn't she?
Sam	*(answers)* Look, I've already said… but if you insist, I'll have full English, no black pudding, two eggs, over easy, beans, fried bread, sausage, tomatoes and definitely no more coffee. *(Hangs up and presses buttons on the phone frantically.)* I put it on silent so we won't be disturbed again.
	(It rings again. Alex goes over and presses the correct button.)
Alex	There. That should stop it.
Sam	*(by way of explanation)* New phone. Not familiar yet. Drink your coffee, Les.
Les	Yes.
Alex	Before it goes cold.
Les	*(swirls coffee around but doesn't drink; thoughtful)* I was wondering, you see…?
Alex	*(dubious)* Yes…?
Les	I thought maybe you're here because you suspect my team of planning to sabotage your green.
	(All three Abbeywood players feign shock.)
Alex	Us…? Think that *you*…?
Sam	No, of course not! Never crossed our minds.

Bobby	But you said…
Alex/Sam	*(quickly)* Shut up, Bobby!
Bobby	I was only saying…
Alex/Sam	*(quickly, louder)* Shut *up*, Bobby!
Les	Because if you were thinking that…
Alex	We weren't.
Sam	Of course not.
Les	I'm afraid I'd have to agree with you. *(Goes to sip coffee.)*
Sam	*(quickly stops Les drinking.)* What did you say?
Les	I suspect they may have a plan to ride BMX bikes across the green and blame the damage on local youths. *(Goes to sip again.)*
Alex	*(stops Les from drinking.)* When?
Les	Tonight. But I can't be sure… they all stopped talking as soon as I was in earshot.
Sam	My God! I was right!
Les	*(goes to sip coffee)* That's why I came here tonight.
	(Sam tries to take Les's coffee away.)
Alex	*(to Sam)* You were.
Les	D'you mind? I'm trying to drink that!
Sam	Bobby'll get you a fresh one. That must be cold by now.
Les	No it's fine.
	(Scuffle ensues while all three wrestle the coffee from Les, who tries to keep it. Ad lib, "I insist", etc. Eventually Bobby ends up with the coffee all over him.)
Bobby	Hell, that's hot!
Alex	No! It was cold. Far too cold.
Sam	Bobby, go and make a fresh one. And wash the evidence out of that mug.
Les	Evidence?
Sam	Slip of the tongue. I meant the grounds.
	(Bobby reluctantly takes the mug inside, brushing off the coffee.)
Sam	Now, you were saying…?

	(Les's phone rings.)
Les	*(answers)* Hello…? Yes…? *(Covers mouthpiece)* I'll have to take this. It's official business. Is there anywhere I can…?
Alex	Use the loo… You know where it is.
Les	Thanks. *(Exits to clubhouse.)*
	(Bobby, entering with a fresh mug of coffee, passes Les in the doorway.)
Alex	So what was all that about? The coffee?
Sam	I put half a pint of *Francsizek's Revenge* in it.
Alex	Why?
Bobby	Excuse me, but what's *Francsizek's Revenge*?
Alex/Sam	*(together)* Shut *up*, Bobby!
Bobby	I was only asking…
Alex	I repeat. Why?
Sam	Because I thought he was here to sabotage us. I thought getting him drunk would get the truth out.
Alex	And now?
Sam	And now he appears to be about to confess something. The last thing we need is the revelation blurred by *Francsizek's Revenge*!
Alex	Ah, I see what you mean.
Sam	So go and make a fresh coffee, Bobby.
	(Bobby has effective been dismissed as Sam and Alex turn to each other to carry on their conversation. Bobby can sell this with expression and body language.)
Bobby	*(the worm starts to turn)* Why me?
Sam	Excuse me?
Bobby	Why me? Why is it always me? Do this, Bobby, do that Bobby… You treat me like a lackey.
Sam	Of course we don't, mate.
Bobby	Don't you mate me… I've had enough!
Sam	Meaning?
Bobby	Meaning I've had enough. Include me or I walk.
Alex	Now, Bobby, you don't mean that.

Bobby	I do mean it, Alex. I've had enough of being treated like a second class member.
Alex	I don't treat you like a second class member, do I?
Bobby	Well, no, but...
Sam	But what?
Bobby	*(rounding on Sam)* But you do!
Sam	*I* do!?
Bobby	Yes!
Sam	I don't. Bobby, you're one of the foundations of the club. Reliable, dependable...
Bobby	And stop trying to butter me up. Like I said. I've had enough.
Sam	You're seriously accusing me of... *(Turns to Alex.)* We don't treat him as a lackey, do we? *(This is more a statement than a genuine question.)*
Alex	Actually, yes, I think we probably do.
Sam	What!?
Bobby	Thank you, Alex.
Sam	I'm speechless.
Alex	Think about it. Bobby's been here with us every night, yes?
Sam	Yes, but...
Alex	And we've had him running round after us, making tea, moving the police car... everything.
Sam	Yes, but...
Alex	And we've excluded him from what's going on.
Sam	Like what?
Bobby	Like this *Francsizek's Revenge* for starters.
Sam	Well, we thought you'd not approve of it.
Alex	To be fair, Sam, *you* decided that, all on your own.
Sam	What is this, have-a-go-at-Sam day?
Bobby	Now you know how it feels.
Sam	I don't believe this.
Bobby	How do you know whether I approve or disapprove unless I know what it is? What was it you said, "The fewer people

	that know about that, the better, especially Bobby. He never could keep a secret"?
Sam	I never said that!
Alex	You did, Sam.
Bobby	And I *heard* you say it. Have you any idea how hurtful that was? *(Silence from Sam.)*
Alex	Sam?
Bobby	Well, *have* you!?
Sam	I... *(Self-realisation)* I'm sorry, Bobby.
Bobby	*(a sneer)* Yes, sure you are.
Sam	I mean it. You're right; I realise that now. I am sorry. Please accept my apology.
Bobby	Very well... But no more *shut up, Bobby*, OK?
Sam	OK. Just one thing, eh?
Bobby	What?
Sam	Please stop saying *"I was only saying"* every second sentence.
Bobby	I don't.
Alex	Sorry, Bobby, but you do.
Bobby	Then I will try to stop. Now, please explain, because I am dying to know... What is *Francsizek's Revenge*?
Sam	Well, you know Francsizek is the groundsman, yes?
Bobby	I figured that bit. But he's on leave. How can he take revenge?
Sam	Have you ever been in his mower shed?
Bobby	Yes.
Sam	And seen that contraption on the bench near the back wall with lots of pipes and a copper cylinder?
Bobby	Oh, the petrol mixer.
Alex	The what?
Bobby	I asked Francsizek what it was one day and he explained it all to me. You pour petrol in the top bit and oil in the bit half way down and it mixes the two together for the mower.

(The others are dumbstruck.)

Sam   And you believed him?

Bobby   Yes. Why not?

Alex   Didn't it occur to you that to mix two-stroke fuel all you have to do is pour oil in with petrol?

Bobby   It all sounded very reasonable when Francsizek explained it. Though I do have trouble with his accent.

Alex   It's a still, Bobby.

Bobby   A what?

Sam   A still. Francsizek's developed a way to make a kind of vodka from grass cuttings.

Bobby   This is a joke, right?

Alex   No joke. He keeps a few bottles in there and sells it to a few customers under the counter. Got it?

Bobby   I think so. All apart from the bit about customers under the counter. What counter? And why are customers under it?

Sam   He means illegally.

Bobby   Wow. Does the Committee know about this?

Sam   Of course they don't! And that's the way it has to stay.

Bobby   *(puts two and two together)* So that copper… It wasn't the woods, was it? You got him drunk!

Sam   Shhh! Keep your voice down! We didn't know he has an alcohol intolerance.

Alex   That's why we need to keep him in the shed until after the match on Saturday.

Bobby   Oh… I see… *(Beat.)* But he's not in the shed.

Alex   What!?

Bobby   I went in a few minutes ago. It's empty.

Sam   Oh no… We've got to find him. And fast!

Bobby   What's the rush if we've got till Saturday?

Sam   Weren't you listening before? Les is the copper's boss! If this gets out we can say goodbye to the League title. We'll be lucky if we don't get chucked in prison.

Bobby   *(blabbering)* But they… he…

Alex   We'd better organise a search party.

Bobby	Here, you didn't give Les any of this vodka, did you?
Alex	Why d'you think Sam insisted on a fresh coffee?
Bobby	Oh, what have you got me into?
Alex	It wasn't my fault!
Bobby	Well it certainly wasn't mine!
Sam	I suppose you're going to blame me!
	(Argument ad lib, until Les returns to the clubhouse door.)
Sam	*(notices Les's return)* Ok, Ok, that will have to do!
Alex	What!?
Sam	*(signals Les is there)* We'll just have to rehearse more.
Bobby	What!?
Sam	For the dramatic society play.
Bobby/Alex	What!?
Sam	Oh, hello, Les. Nothing wrong I hope?
Alex	Ah…
Les	Wrong?
Sam	You had a phone call. Alex and Bobby and I… All three of us… decided to use the time to go through our lines. For the play… At the dramatic society. Didn't we?
	(Dumb nods from the others.)
Les	I didn't know you were *in* a dramatic society.
Sam	Oh, yes… Love treading the boards, don't we?
	(Dumb nods from the others.)
Les	What is it?
Sam	What's what?
Les	The play. What play are you doing?
Sam	Ah…
Alex	Er…
Bobby	It's called *Francsizek's Revenge*. A policeman gets kidnapped and held hostage.
Alex	*(sotto voce)* Bobby!
Sam	But not at a bowling green.
Alex	No, at a…

Sam	…a football stadium.
Alex	In South America.
Sam	Miles from here.
Les	I don't think I've heard of it. Who wrote it?
Alex	Er… That Welsh playwright. What's her name?
Bobby	Ann!
Les	Ann who?
Sam	Ann Onymous.
Les	You'll have to let me know the dates. We'll organise a trip to see it.
Alex	Anyway, your phone call…?
Les	Our constable. Officially missing.
Alex	Oh, God.
Bobby	I er… More coffee. *(Dashes off.)*
Sam	Coward! *(Turns and smiles to Les.)* I'm sure there's nothing wrong. Probably had a couple of beers and is sleeping it off somewhere.
Les	Well, I hope so. We're mobilising search teams.
Alex	Isn't that a bit extreme?
Les	Well, there's a problem. He's diabetic.
Sam	As well?
Les	Sorry? As well as what?
Alex	As well as missing.
Les	If he doesn't get regular food and drink he could slip into a coma.
Alex	Oh, heck. That's serious.
Sam	*(calls)* Bobby! Did you make that coffee?
Bobby	*(enters with coffees)* OK, I'm coming! *(Brings out coffees and hands them round.)* Sam, can I have a word with you please?
Sam	What now?
Bobby	In private?
Sam	That's not very polite, Bobby.
Bobby	No. Sorry. It's about my… It's personal.

Les	Don't mind me.
	(Bobby and Sam talk near the clubhouse door - very animatedly, while Alex continues to distract Les.)
Alex	So…, you're concerned your bowlers are going to come tonight?
Les	Yes. I don't see how I can continue as chairperson if I don't have their trust.
Alex	So what will you do?
Les	I was wondering if I could join you.
Alex	Join us? Abbeywood?
	(This exclamation attracts the attention of Sam and Bobby, who come over.)
Sam	What's that? You want to join Abbeywood?
Les	If you'll have me.
Sam	But you're the chairman.
Bobby	And we've already got a chairman.
Les	As a bowler, not as chairman.
Sam	You're a fantastic bowler.
Les	I'm a bit rusty.
Bobby	With you on our team we'd walk away with the league title.
Les	No, that's impossible. I'd still be registered with West Worth. I wouldn't be able to play until next season.
Bobby	Couldn't we bend the rules?
Les	Bobby, I'm a senior police officer, duty-bound to uphold the law, whether I agree with it or not.
Bobby	Oh.
Les	It doesn't matter what it is, from driving offences through theft, violence… Anything illegal I have to clamp down on it.
Bobby	What, even if…
Alex	Bobby, don't…
Les	Even if what?
Bobby	Even if, hypothetically speaking of course, someone was, what…? Making illegal booze in their sheds?
Les	It's still an offence. And I would still have to investigate.

Sam	*(laughing it off)* But who would do that round here, Bobby? We're not in the backwoods of America now.
Bobby	I was only saying…
Sam	Anyway, back to the subject. I'm sure I can speak for all the members when I say of course we'd be proud to have you, Les.
Les	Thank you. I shall resign tomorrow, at the same time expressing my concerns about my suspicions. I feel you at Abbeywood have acted honourably throughout…
Sam	Oh yes, we have… *(To Alex and Bobby)* Haven't we?
Alex/Bobby	Oh yes.
Les	Whereas those at West Worth have not.
Sam/Alex/Bobby	*(though not in unison)* No.
	(Les's phone rings again.)
Les	May I? (Indicating he wants to go inside for privacy.
Alex	Help yourself.
	(Sam, Alex & Bobby watch as Les exits into the clubhouse.)
Alex	I can't believe it!
Sam	What a result! The best player they'd have in years and joining us. We'll sweep away all the opposition.
	(As they are talking, Pat sways on from DL, unnoticed at first.)
Bobby	Shame we have to wait for registration, though. Isn't there any way we can fiddle registration?
Alex	You mean falsify it? No way. You heard what he said about honesty and the rules. This season will be down to us to win. Losing Les, though - it's bound to dent their confidence, especially when their chairman and best player's leaving under a cloud.
Pat	Eshcuse me. Can you tell me where the main reshtaurant is pleash?
Sam	Pat! How did you get out?
Alex	*(to Bobby)* I thought you locked him away somewhere.
Bobby	I did. The mower shed.
Sam	What!?

Bobby   Seemed like a good idea at the time.

Alex   But that's where Francsizek makes his er… *(Checks Les is out of earshot)* medicine.

Bobby   I thought it was vodka.

Sam   It *is* vodka, you idiot!

Bobby   But I thought Alex said…?

Alex   At this rate Pat won't be sober enough to go on holiday till he comes back!

Sam   What are we going to do? Les could be back any minute.

Pat   I think I'm going to be ill… *(Sways.)*

Alex   Quick, get him to the chairs.

Pat   Don't undershtand… Never suffered sea sickness before.

Sam   Well, it is very choppy, old chap.

              (They all help Pat to a chair stage L. Bobby moves the jack and mat so the others can sit Pat down.)

Bobby   Remove one jack, replace it with another.

Sam   Enough of your terrible jokes, Bobby, OK?

Pat   Hair of the dog. *(Tries to stand, unsuccessfully.)* Thash what I need!

Sam   We think you've had enough hairs and dogs, Pat.

Pat   Bloody Mary. Works wonders.

Bobby   *(genuinely)* Bloody Mary? Who's she? *(Puts the bowls mat down but keeps the jack in hand, "weighing it" by tossing it up very slightly.)*

Sam   What!? *(Sarcastic)* The landlady of the Packet Inn.

Bobby   Packet Inn? Don't get it.

Sam   You will if you don't pack it in.

Bobby   I was only asking…

              (Les can be heard finishing a phone call as he approaches the clubhouse door.)

Les   OK, but keep me informed, OK?

Alex   Quick! Les!

              (Bobby grabs a blanket from one of the chairs and throws it over Pat, who is still upright. All three stand between the door and the chairs, attempting to hide Pat's presence.

Bobby is furthest left, near the back of the seats.)

Les	Yes… I'm likely to be up all night. *(Enters from clubhouse door.)*
Sam	Les! Welcome back!
Alex	Everything all right?
Les	Not really. They still haven't heard from Pat. And his mobile's been switched off now. *(Drifts down to them, nearer the seat where Pat is.)*
Sam	Probably nothing to worry about. I mean, what could have happened?
Les	Pat's usually so punctual. *(Notices Pat in the seat.)* What's that?
Sam	(crowding together with the others) What's what?
Les	On that seat.
Sam	Nothing. I can't see anything, can you? *(This to Bobby and Alex, who both shake their heads and try to keep up the shield.)*
Les	There's something suspicious going on here. Out of my way!
	(Pushes them apart and looks at the form under the blanket.)
Sam	*(in total synchronisation)* It's the new mower
Alex	It's the new groundsman.
Les	No surprises for guessing who this is!. *(Takes the seat next to Pat and slowly lifts the blanket.)* It's Pat!
Pat	*(slurring)* Hello guvnor. What are you doing on the ship?
Les	What's he doing under a blanket?
Bobby	*(weakly)* Under-cover police work?
Les	And I thought you lot could be trusted!
	(Les turns to look at Sam and Alex accusingly. Bobby knocks him out with the jack.)
Alex	*(aghast)* Bobby!
Sam	*Now* what have you done?
Bobby	Well, I just thought…
Sam	But you *didn't* think, did you?

Bobby	We have to keep it all a secret till after the match on Saturday.
Alex	By kidnapping the police!?
Bobby	One more won't make much difference.
Sam	No, why don't you ring up the station and see if they can send a few more down? See if we can complete our collection.
Bobby	Sorry.
Alex	What are we going to do?
Sam	I'm thinking about it. *(Sits R.)*
Alex	*(sits next to Sam)* I'll help.
Bobby	And I...
Sam/Alex	*(quickly interrupting)* You will do nothing!
Bobby	But I...
Sam	Nothing! Go and make some coffee.
Alex	Hang on. We'll have to move them first.
Sam	Where to?
Alex	There's only one place we can hope to hide them - the mower shed.
Sam	Is that wise? We're already going down for kidnap and GBH, we don't need to add making illegal booze to the list.
Alex	Any other suggestions?
Sam	*(reluctantly)* No. None.
Alex	Come on then... Let's get them in there before someone else turns up. Bobby, you go and make sure there's no more booze in there.
Bobby	Right.

(Bobby exits as Sam and Alex start to move the bodies off.)

Curtain

ACT II Scene 2

Scene	the same - Saturday afternoon.

It is midway through the repeat bowling match. The arrangement is exactly as the start of the play.

Alex and Bobby are seated stage R, and Chris and Joe, West Worth supporters, stage L, all holding scorecards and pens, with small wooden boards to support the scorecards and a bulldog clip to keep each in place. Bowls and bags are on the floor around them. The door and windows to the clubhouse are open, as befits the summer's day. Sam enters from the clubhouse. At the rear of the hall, Nick (Abbeywood) and Nat (West Worth) enter.

Nat	*(calls to Joe)* How much am I short?
Joe	You ought to know, you're closer to it. Bowl up, for God's sake!
Nat	Not helpful, Sam; we're all trying.
Alex	It's like an exact replay of the last match.
Bobby	Just as close, too.
Sam	We couldn't possibly draw again… Could we?
Alex	I hope not. I don't think I could live through the last week again.
Sam	How are our… guests?
Alex	Pat is still enjoying a life on the ocean waves. Les keeps falling asleep.
Bobby	Concussion, probably.
Alex	I still think we should have called an ambulance.
Bobby	So do I.
Sam	*(turns on Bobby)* That's rich, coming from you.
Bobby	I was only saying…
Sam	If it hadn't been for you we'd have only had one hostage.
Alex	Doesn't really matter now, does it? We're all accessories.
Bobby	We can say we all lost our memories and didn't know what we were doing.
Sam	You don't know what you're doing anyway.
Alex	I keep playing though in my mind what we're going to say when it's all over.
Sam	And…?
Alex	"Help" is all I can think of.
Sam	Let's win this match first, eh?

Joe	*(looking towards Nat)* Two? That's game! *(Marks card and detaches it from the board.)*
	(All clap as Nick and Nat walk to the stage carrying their bowls, a jack and a mat. They shake hands as they get close.)
Nat	Well played. I thought I had you there.
Nick	Same here. You were unlucky. Shame it couldn't have been a draw, eh? Well played anyway.
Nat	He's still a cheat. Glad I won.
Nick	He cheated. Otherwise I'd have won.
Alex/Joe	*(together)* It's winning that counts.
Bobby	Remember when we used to say it's winning that counts?
Sam	I've had enough of this! No more Mr Nice Guy!
Bobby	What're you going to do?
Sam	Watch and learn. *(Moves to the West Worth side.)* Coffee? Tea?
Nat	Yes, thanks. No sugar for me, though, I'm on a diet.
Sam	Yes, you should be.
Nat	What's that supposed to mean?
Sam	Skip it. Right, coffees coming up.
	(Sam disappears into the clubhouse and we see him making drinks through the window. Very quickly, Sam returns carrying four mugs of coffee.)
Joe	That was quick.
	(Each takes the offered coffee.)
Chris	*(after tasting it)* Ugh! It's stone cold! What's going on.
Sam	Couldn't find any bleach.
Nat	Is this supposed to be funny?
Sam	Not in the least. You're up to something. I don't know what it is but I want it stopped. Now!
Alex	*(coming across to Sam)* Sam! What are you doing? Come over here and calm down. *(Pulls him away.)*
Sam	I've had enough, Alex.
Alex	Bobby, will you get our friends from West Worth some fresh coffee please?

Bobby	Sure.
Nat	Fresh *warm* coffee?
	(Bobby collects the cups and exits to the clubhouse. We see him making drinks through the window.)
Alex	Sit down, Sam.
Sam	*(tries to get to the West Worth team again)* I don't want to sit down. I want...
Alex	*(forceful)* I said sit down, Sam. *(Forces Sam into a seat.)* Now what was all that about?
	(The West Worth team chat among themselves so do not overhear the next conversation between Alex and Sam.)
Sam	I've had enough of their cheating, sneering, superior comments.
Alex	I thought you wanted us to win the League?
Sam	I do, but...
Alex	We're hardly going to win if you start weighing into our guests.
Sam	Guests? Hah!
Alex	Opposition, then. Will that do?
Sam	I just saw red.
Alex	You're playing right into their hands, Sam. If they can provoke you into something rash, they make a complaint to the League and we get banned. Is that what you want?
Sam	No, of course not.
Alex	Then just calm down.
Sam	It's lack of sleep. I reckon I'll sleep for a week when this is over.
Alex	*(dry)* No. I hear prison cell beds aren't all that comfortable.
Sam	That's not funny, Alex.
Alex	Our little problems haven't gone away.
Sam	Very quiet though, aren't they?
Alex	Bobby keeps feeding them mugs of coffee made half and half with *Francsizek's Revenge*. They have no idea what day it is.
Sam	I bet they will when they sober up. Bobby doesn't think things through most of the time.

Alex   I think he's on to something with this one. We keep them on the cruise ship until Sunday afternoon…

Sam   They're *both* on the cruise ship!?

Alex   Yup. Pat's cruising the Caribbean and Les's doing Alaska. It makes for some interesting conversations. Did you know they have humpback whales in the coast off Jamaica?

Sam   So what happens on Sunday…? According to Bobby's plan, I mean.

Alex   When it gets dark we put them in the car and drive them to the sea front. One final shot of *Francsizek's Revenge* and they'll sleep until dawn.

Sam   And then?

Alex   And then we just have to hope it's all a surreal dream.

Sam   There are some holes in Bobby's plan.

Alex   Enough to strain your greens through. But have you got a better one?

Sam   Not exactly. I suppose it would be our word against theirs.

Alex   True. And there's three of us versus two of them.

Sam   I'm sure there are one or two other club members who'd back us if needed.

Alex   Only as a last resort. The fewer people who know about this, the better

Nat   *(calling across; a taunt)* All right over there?.

Sam   *(rising)* I'd still like to wipe that smug smile of Nat's face.

Nat   I told you; it's what they want. Go and take a walk along the lane, calm down a bit. Come on, I'll come with you.

         (Alex and Sam rise and go to the clubhouse door.)

Alex   *(calls to Bobby)* Bobby…! Those coffees ready yet?

Bobby   *(from by the window)* Just coming.

         (Alex and Sam disappear.)

Nat   Keep at them. Sam nearly cracked then.

Chris   I thought he was going to thump you.

Nat   If it takes a black eye to win the title, *(dramatically)* I'm prepared to make the sacrifice.

         (Bobby enters unnoticed from the clubhouse carrying a tray of four coffees.)

Nick	I'm surprised Les hasn't put in an appearance. He should be here representing the club.
	(Bobby stops dead at the mention of Les's name, listening.)
Nat	Les's been behaving a bit odd recently. Not part of the group, if you know what I mean.
Joe	I heard a rumour he's thinking of packing it all in and joining this lot.
Bobby	*(turns to the door, going back just inside. Sotto voce)* Alex…! Sam…!
Nick	That's the last thing we need. Our best player joining our worst enemies.
Bobby	A mean lot, aren't they?
Joe	The development fund you mean?
	(Bobby comes back out and listens again.)
Nat	Despicable bunch. I'm sure they must have a few coppers hidden away somewhere.
	(Bobby looks aghast and has an intake of breath. Chris notices Bobby.)
Chris	Ah, the coffees!
	(Bobby is frozen.)
Nat	Bobby… The coffees?
Bobby	What?
Nat	Coffees… While they're still hot.
	(Chris and Joe rise and hand the coffees out between them while Bobby stands dumbstruck, holding the tray.)
Bobby	Coffees.
Nat	Thanks, Bobby.
Bobby	Yes… coffees.
Nat	Any biscuits?
Bobby	What?
Nat	Biscuits?
Bobby	*(rambling)* Sandwiches… inside… cakes… biscuits… yes.
Nat	I think Bobby's finally lost it. Anyone want some grub?
	(The West Worth players go into the clubhouse out of

sight. Bobby still stands dumbstruck.)

Bobby	*(rambling)* Sandwiches... cakes... biscuits... coppers... Oh hell!
	(Alex and Sam enter, Alex has his arm around EDDY.)
Alex	Feeling better now?
Sam	I suppose. But I warn you... one more word.
Alex	*(notices Bobby's spaced-out expression.)* All right, Bobby?
Bobby	*(rambling)* Sandwiches... cakes... biscuits...
Sam	What?
Alex	Bobby, what's wrong?
Bobby	They know!
Sam	Who knows?
Bobby	West Worth. They know!
Alex	Know what?
Bobby	That we've got the police hostages.
Sam	Hardly *hostages...*
Alex	What makes you think that?
Bobby	I came out with the coffees and heard them.
Alex	What did they say?
Bobby	That we're a despicable bunch...
Sam	Typical!
Bobby	And that we must have a few policemen hidden away somewhere.
Sam	What?
Alex	How could they have found out.
Bobby	And they know Les's thinking of joining us too.
Sam	There must be a mole in the club.
Alex	But who? Apart from the three of us, nobody else knows.
	(Suspicion all round.)
Sam	Unless someone's been in the mower shed without us knowing.
Alex	They can't. It's locked. And Bobby's got the only key. *(Pause.)* You have still got the key, Bobby.
	(A look of concern on Bobby's face. He searches pockets

in a panic.)

Sam   Bobby!

(Eventually the key is found.)

Bobby   Here! Here it is!

Alex   And nobody's borrowed it?

Bobby   No. No way.

Sam   And you've not leant it to anyone?

Bobby   Do I look stupid?

Sam   Well...

Alex   No, of course you don't. And that's the only key?

Bobby   Apart from the one Francsizek has, yes.

Sam   What if Francsizek came home early? Where did he go away to? And please don't say a cruise!

Alex   To his sister's.

Bobby   In Poland?

Alex   No. Peterborough.

Sam   So it's possible he's come back early?

Alex   Possible. But if he had, and he had found two unwanted guests in his mower shed, he would have complained to Sam, as chairman.

Sam   True. Never slow in complaining, is Francsizek.

Bobby   Which brings us back to a mole.

Alex   Well, if it's a mole, it's one of the three of us.

Bobby   *(all three together, ad lib)* Well it isn't me!
Sam   *(all three together, ad lib)* You're not accusing me, I hope!
Alex   *(all three together, ad lib)* ...and it's not me!

(They share suspicious looks at each other.)

Sam   This is ridiculous.

Alex   And not our first priority. Suggestions anyone?

Bobby   We could move them out of the shed.

Sam   Ridiculous! Where to?

Bobby   I was only saying...

Alex   No use in broad daylight. Your previous master plan will have to do.

Sam	We just have to bluff it out.
Bobby	*(hearing noises)* Shhh! They're coming back.
Alex	Say nothing!
	(Chris, Joe, Nick and Nat all appear carrying plastic plates with sandwiches and cakes. They look curiously at the guilt-ridden Abbeywood team.)
Alex	*(false smile)* Enjoying it, are we?
Nat	Not especially.
Chris	*(suddenly suspicious of the food)* Aren't you having any?
Sam	In a bit. You enjoy yours.
Joe	Why' what's up with them?
Bobby	Nothing's up with them. Made them myself this morning.
Nick	(thrusts plate forward.) You eat one then.
Bobby	OK, OK. *(Reaches for sandwich.)*
Sam	*(stops Bobby)* Wait a minute. What are you accusing us of here?
Nat	Nothing. Everything!
Chris	I wouldn't put it past you to have poisoned them.
Alex	Oh, come on. You're being ridiculous now.
Joe	"Anything to win," right!?
Alex	But poisoning your tea? How paranoid can you get?
Nat	*(bristling)* Are you accusing us of being paranoid?
Sam	*(up for a fight)* Are you accusing us of being mass murderers?
Bobby	Oh, this is pathetic. *(Grabs a sandwich and eats it.)* There! I've eaten one.
Nick	Hey! That was mine!
Sam	*(happy to continue the fight)* Are you accusing us of stealing now?
Nat	Yes! We are!
Sam	In that case…
	(Sam takes a cake from one of the plates and pushes it into Nat's face. There follows a complete bunfight, with both teams hurling food at each other. Les and Pat stagger and sway on, not aware of the fight, managing to

catch the odd sandwich. They sit to eat.)

Les   *(looking out)* Nice day, isn't it?

Pat   Sea's as calm as a millpond.

(Pause - then Pat starts to scratch.)

Les   Something itching?

Pat   Yes. My arm.

Les   *(joins in)* Me too.

(The mayhem continues as the lights fade to black.)

End of ACT II Scene 2

Epilogue

Scene   *the same, half an hour later. Apart from the remains of the food fight the stage is empty. The portable radio fades in.*

RADIO   …the dramatic scene at the Abbeywood bowling club earlier today where missing police officers Les Evans and Pat Riley were discovered locked in a garage apparently drugged by person or persons unknown. Police are unable to issue a full statement until the pair have fully recovered, but a spokesman told his programme that they are on the lookout for a West Indian or Alaskan gang.

By an incredible coincidence, while still on the subject of bowling, the top-of-the-league match between local rivals Abbeywood and West Worth Bowling Clubs was abandoned earlier today after a fight broke out. Both teams have been taken into custody pending investigations. An emergency meeting by officials of the Bowling League has, therefore, awarded the title to the third-placed club, Rackton BC.

Now we go across to Janet for tomorrow's weather…

Curtain

Furniture and Properties
ACT I Scene 1

Set   Lines of chairs on the verandah, facing audience
Scorecards & pens, with small wooden boards & bulldog clips
Money box or collection box *(on the floor L)*
Bowls and bags are on the floor around them. The door and windows to the clubhouse are open, as befits the summer's day.
Modified bowls bag *(on floor)*

Page 3   Bowls, a jack and a mat *(Nick and Nat)*

Page 5   Change *(Nat, in pocket)*

Page 6   Tray with cup and saucer, teaspoon & plate of biscuits/cakes. *(Sam - in clubhouse)*
Debris *(Sam, on head and shoulders)*
Bowling wood *(Sam, in clubhouse)*

ACT I Scene 2

Page 10   Portable radio
Small torch *(Bobby, in pocket)*
Large torch *(Alex, in clubhouse)*
3 mugs of coffee *(Sam, in clubhouse)*
Camera *(Sam, round neck)*

Page 11   Bottle/flask of vodka with no label *(Sam, in pocket/handbag)*
Mobile phone *(Sam, in pocket/handbag)*

Page 15   Torch *(Pat)*

Page 18   Bowling wood *(Bobby, in clubhouse)*

Page 24   Car keys *(Pat, in pocket)*

Page 27   £5 and £10 bank notes *(Alex, in pocket)*

Page 27   Two 10p pieces *(Sam, in pocket)*

Page 28   Pizza box with pizza *(Bobby, in the clubhouse)*

Page 30   Torch *(Les)*

Page 30   Pieces of wood *(Sam, off L)*

Page 32   2 unlabelled full bottles of booze (water) *(Pat, off L)*

ACT II Scene 1

Page 34   Add mobile phone *(under chairs L)*
Tray and four mugs *(Sam, in clubhouse)*
Bowls jack and a mat *(on chair L)*
Sweeteners - *(Les, in pocket/handbag)*
Tray and four mugs
Bowls jack and a mat *(on the chair L)*

Page 37   Flask of booze *(Sam, in pocket)*

Page 40   Mug of coffee *(Bobby, in clubhouse)*

Page 46   Tray of coffee *(Bobby, in clubhouse)*

ACT II Scene 2

Page 52   Set as start of ACT I Scene 1 *(need not be identical)*

Page 54   Tray with 4 mugs coffee *(Sam, in clubhouse)*

Page 56   Tray with 4 mugs coffee *(Bobby, in clubhouse)*

Page 59   Padlock key *(Bobby, in pocket)*

Page 60   Plates of buffet food *(in clubhouse)*

Lighting

ACT I Scene 1

Page 3   General summer daylight

ACT I Scene 2

Page 10   Late evening lighting (dark and grows darker over the course of the scene)

ACT II Scene 1

Page 34   Night time.

ACT II Scene 2

Page 52   Afternoon lighting

62

Sound Effects
ACT I Scene 1

Cue 1   Clatter as the bowl strikes something. - **Page 7**
Cue 1a   Crash of broken glass backstage

ACT I Scene 2

Cue 2   Portable radio plays some night music softly. - **Page 10**
Cue 3   Radio off - **Page 10**
             Cue **Bobby** OK, OK... I get the message!
Cue 4   Crash in clubhouse (Les falling) - **Page 18**
             Cue **Sam** Well, we can't undo what's done.
Cue 5   Car horn (off) - **Page 26**
             Cue **Bobby** I was only saying...

ACT II Scene 1

Cue 6   Les's mobile phone rings - **Page 35**
             Cue **Sam** Help...? Us...?
Cue 7   Pat's mobile phone rings - **Page 37**
             Cue **Les** I told the station to keep trying the mobile. He's not answering it for some reason.
Cue 8   Pat's phone rings again - **Page 38**
             Cue **Sam** Just a joke. My daughter. Wants to know if I want a meal when I get in.
Cue 9   Les's phone rings - **Page 40**
             Cue **Sam** Now, you were saying...?
Cue 10   Les's phone rings again - **Page 48**
             Cue **Sam, Alex & Bobby** No.

Epilogue

Cue 11   Radio announcement - as script - **Page 62**

Other plays by Ian Hornby - see www.scripts4theatre.com

Abanazar's Revenge	Jayne with a Y
Aladdin dot com	Late of This Address
'Allo, 'Allo, 'Allo, (Est There Any Body La)?	Mind Games
Are You Sure There's No Body There?	Murdered, Presumed Dead
Be Careful Who You Wish For	No, Minister
Boomerang	One Across
The Cat's Away	The Price to Pay
Cinderella	A Question of Innocence
Cold Blood	Remember Me
Conference Pairs	Robin Hood
The Dark Side of the Son	Shades of Blue
D I Why?	Situation Vacant
A Dish Served Cold	Tied Up at the Office
Do You Keep Stationery?	To Sleep, Perchance
Dream, Lover!	Voices
The Ex Factor	Wait Until the Ghost is Clear
An Eye for an Eye, Darling	Where There's a Will...
Hello, Is There Any Body There?	Whispers
Help! I'm a Celebrity Pantomime Dame; Get Me Out of Here!	Whose Line Was It, Anyway?
The Hex Factor	Why Won't They Believe Me?
Jack Up!	The Winter of Discontent

Printed in Great Britain
by Amazon